CW01590174

INTRODUCTION

Welcome to this my eighth book in the *"Around"* series, which has been brought out in [illegible] sister book *"Oldland and the Surrounding Parishes."* and is designed to replace *Oldland Then & Now* which was first published in 1996.As the title describes, the earlier book compared certain views of the village at the beginning and end of the twentieth century, whereas in this book I have included many more older pictures, the majority of which have not previously been published, or certainly published in this format. Scattered in between those pictures are photographs taken during the 1980's a decade that has already become part of our history, but is close enough for the younger generation to have a chance to reminisce. Hopefully the reader will see from this book that a considerable part of Oldland at the start of the twentieth century has hardly changed, but with the growth of the area over the past forty years or so, there are parts of the village that today are totally unrecognisable with Oldland of eighty years ago. Probably the most noticeable change that has taken place to the whole village is the amount of traffic either parked along the streets, or rushing through without a second glance. The clock cannot of course be put back, but on the enclosed pages it will be possible for you to take a glimpse of the slower pace of life once enjoyed by our forbearers and to see how, despite their poverty, how proud they were of the area in which they lived, no rubbish or litter thrown away for all to see, no graffiti, neatly trimmed hedgerows, and an absence of excessive street furniture that now adds to the overall statute vandalism that blights our environment.

In producing this book I have arranged for it to link in with my *"Around Bitton"* to the south, *"Longwell Green ~ Our Village"* to the west, and *"Around Kingswood"* and *"Around Warmley"* for the other points of the compass, and these and all my books are highly recommended for those who are interested in a wider area of this corner of South Gloucestershire.

During the preparation of this book I have received invaluable help from Mike Tozer, Janet and Derek Fisher, Andrew Palmer, Rosemary Rainbird and others who have allowed me to include pictures from their individual collections, and to Sheila Brooks for reading through the transcript. Sadly although my late wife Doreen assisted in its early preparation, her untimely death has meant that she was unable to see the end product. Throughout this book I have endeavoured to minimize any mistakes made but should any exist then they are unfortunately of my own making, for which I apologize and trust that any such errors will not distract you from enjoying the remaining contents.

Ian S Bishop

December 2005

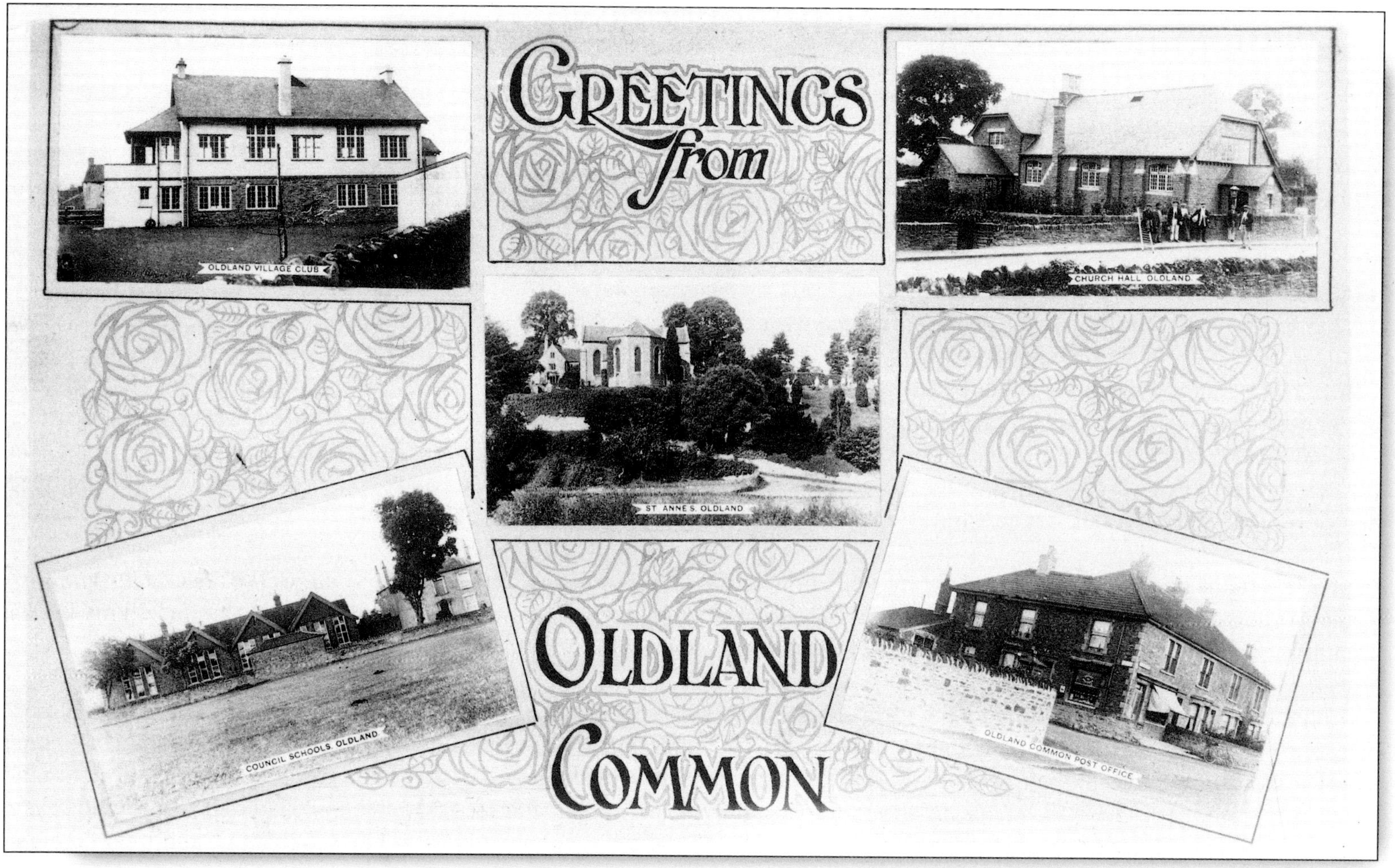

An interesting and rare Greetings Card of Oldland Common showing five small photographs all taken in the village around 1920.

The rural nature of Tower Road South and the approach to Oldland is demonstrated in this view as a lone cyclist struggles up the rise towards the cameraman from where the road crossed Warmley Brook. With the sun reflecting on its frontage, the *Collier's Arms* is the prominent building on the left, whilst less conspicuous are the backs of the cottages as they cluster up Cowhorn Hill. c1910.

West Street in 1914 at a time when it was perfectly safe, for those who wished to have their picture taken, to stand in the middle of the road without a care in the world. The late summer sunshine bathes the rank of houses, as the female house owners exchanged the daily news, and may already be expressing their concern over the possibility of an impending war.

Other houses are yet to be built as is the construction of the pavement, and it will be many years before the recently invented internal combustion engine will take over. Note the dog resting in the shade. There is a gap of about eighty-five years between both pictures on this page, and whilst the sun is still reflected by the same rank of houses, many other changes have taken place, and no longer does West Street have the calm of a rural community, as modern traffic rushes by.

Charles Carr, Sycamore Stores, Oldland Common nr. Bristol.

Mr Charles Carr is pictured with his wife outside his Sycamore Stores at number 39 West Street. As can be seen by the proud sign above the door, he traded as a grocer, draper and provision merchant, from his little shop, which was probably something akin to an Aladdin's cave inside. With the property now converted to a private house, this picture was taken around 1907.

On the left are Sybil and Brenda Robbins standing outside their home at 108 West Street in 1930, whilst on the right are the Lewis children at 118 West Street around 1911 when their home doubled up as the local Registrar of Births and Deaths office. Below the date stone the board shows that J B Burton is the Registrar for the Bitton District, and that he was there on Mondays from 11.00am to 1.00pm

At the time when this picture was taken around 1922, both the Methodist Chapel and the Village Hall were relatively new buildings in the village, and no doubt when the photographer arrived he created a fair amount of interest as shown by the number of the villagers who were anxious to ensure that their image and that of their children was fixed for posterity. To the left, behind the wall, is the area that was once occupied by the Common, before it was enclosed and subsequently built upon.

The Whitsunday procession, once a very familiar sight in the area, winds its way on a bright summer's day along West Street past the junction with Court Road, with a Shell filling station on the corner, and past the village hall at a time when it was being used as a warehouse to store furniture. In the picture below the local vicar of St Annes, the Rev Thomas leads the procession, Travelling in style on one of J H Upward's lorries are Margaret Gregory; Susan Jelf; Jane Purnell; Julia Hall; Nick Tarrant; David Bishop, and Andrew Batt c1968

No longer a petrol filling station, the corner shop has now become the Oldland Fruit Market & Garden Centre, with its own "pull-in" presently occupied by a Ford Popular 351PHT. A light dusting of snow decorates the front garden, whilst an A-frame listing the many goods available for sale tries to catch the attention of those who pass by. February 1986.

Three different views of the Village Hall with, top left, the celebrations surrounding the laying of the foundation stone, top right the view of the back as it was originally built. Bottom left is another one of the "posed" photographs showing the frontage, a small group of village ladies, a school boy and cycle an ostler with a horse that did not want to keep its head still and, behind the hall is the scout hut c1922.

Many soldiers of the First World War were brought back to local hospitals and rehabilitation centres to convalesce, with part of their treatment being provided by the supportive civilian population who organised parties, such as the one held at the newly constructed Village Hall on the 12th August 1916. On the right, next to the boy with his hand on his hip are the twins Jack and Clara Lovell from North Street, Oldland Common.

On the left a very rural looking West Street stretches out in front of us as seen from the railway bridge around 1911. To the left is the entrance to the forecourt of the *Greyhound* public house, and behind the central tree the newly built Methodist Chapel can be seen, whilst on the right is the "enclosed" common. Below left is the same view taken some 83 years later, whilst below is a close-up of the left-hand buildings when the modernised shop traded as Oldland stores

Looking down The Clamp towards the junction with High Street from the railway bridge on the 26th May 1990. The haulage firm, G L Baker are still operating out of the transport yard adjacent to the railway, although this will not last for much longer, and for safety reasons The Clamp has been made one-way to prevent vehicles joining West Street close to the brow of the railway bridge "hump."

On the same day a Badgerline Bristol built single-deck bus No 1331 ~ OAE953M enters West Street from the High Street on route 558 only to find that there is an interloper parked at the bus stop. The *Cherry Tree Inn* is on the right, and behind the tree a glimpse of Mr Morgan's cottage can just be seen.

Although a poor quality picture of circa 1950, this is the only view known to the author of the *Greyhound Inn* when it was still in operation. In addition to the standing sign, the inn's name and the brewers name board can be seen above the upstairs' windows. Mr Gerrish, a previous landlord, at one time used the single storey building in the background as a slaughterhouse, and between the wars it formed part of a smallholding for pigs.

Sometime during the late 1950's, the left-hand side of the building was demolished whilst the remaining portion was converted into a cottage. However, on the 13th April 1984 there was a serious fire in the top half of the building, causing its ultimate demise.

Not quite "ye olde smithy" on the left, but George Jefferies at his workshop at 47 West Street could turn his hand to most jobs that involved metal and plenty of strength c 1920.

On the right a general view of West Street from the railway bridge c1995.

The original *Union Inn* stood at ninety degrees to the present *Union Inn* [now known as the *Cherry Tree*] with West Street to the right of the picture and cottages on the left c1905.

Before the adjacent Cowhorn Hill was widened, there was a rank of cottages in North Street at the junction with both these roads. During the early 1950's, the end cottage in particular under went some extensive restoration, whilst *Rose Cottage* on the right looks as though it needs to be next on the list. Behind that cottage it is possible to glimpse the side of the *Crown & Horseshoe* public house.

The producer of this card has wrongly stated that this is West Street when quite clearly the cottages and the adjacent *Crown & Horse Shoe Inn* are in North Street. Taken in 1914, Mr Garth Short leans on his gatepost outside the smallest of the three attached cottages, whilst next-door Violet and Cathy Phelps are determined to get into the picture

This charming picture of the *Crown & Horse Shoe Inn* in its sylvan setting, although already one of the gnarled elms can no longer offer the resting traveller any shade. With outside steps leading up to the Assembly Rooms and railings around her window gardens, Mrs Winifred Elliot ruled the roost as she served the locals, and the occasional passer-by with a refreshing beverage c1937

The villagers of Oldland Common celebrate the end of the European theatre of World War Two in 1945; with many of the children in fancy dress the photographer has arranged the group at the side entrance to the *Crown & Horse Shoe*. Note the depth of the West Street cottages.

On the right is the substantial No 9 *The Elms* North Street in its winter mode, as we look back along North Street, towards the *Crown & Horse Shoe Inn* and the rank of cottages around 1967. Some ten years latter, *The Elms* was demolished to make way for the entrance to Pennine Road. Studying the second picture of North Street [see below] taken from the junction with Cloverlea Road enables the exact position of this house to be more

readily identified as the left-hand ivy-covered corner can be seen on the right. It is also possible to see why No.9 was so named with a spectacular group of Elms partially shielding the Inn With just a solitary bicycle parked at the curb when it was safe to do so, this charming view was fixed in time around 1930, although once again the photographer has put an incorrect caption on the picture.

On a beautifully hot summer's day, Doreen and Jill Bishop stroll along Cloverlea Road past the site of the old doctor's [Dr W John] surgery, and on their way towards the houses bottom left 20 July 1986. Below right is the old Cloverlea Road Chapel building 24 December 1990. Demolished in the following year to make way for houses in Cook Close.

On a bright summer's day around 1910, a photographer arrived in the village proceeded to set up his equipment and to compose his pictures, no doubt carefully choosing an area where local residents and children had gathered as, not only did the people help to animate the pictures and to make them more interesting, but there was also a great chance that some of those who had been photographed might end up buying a copy.

Stanford's (Bristol) Ltd., had for many years, its furniture making factory at 31-35 North Street as seen above on the 20th July 1986, and a little later top right on Christmas Eve 1990, with their van A956UHT parked up for the forthcoming holiday. No doubt the cost of making furniture became more and more expensive, whilst the value of the land on which the factory stood appreciated to the extent that two years later the site was sold for development, as demonstrated by the lower picture, taken in June 1993, showing that the cleared site had been acquired by the developers Midas Construction Ltd., for the building of Cook Close.

Also taken in June 1993, this is a different perspective of the same area that was once the home of Stanford's Offices and factory, and is now the site of Cook Close. Note in the left-hand wall the filled-in position of a letterbox.

This is one of the original small cottages that formerly faced onto the common land, Number 47 North Street, bathed in the winter sunshine Christmas Eve 1990.

Although a sturdy stone wall encloses this field, it once formed the common land that gave our village its name. When this picture was taken an architectural mixture of villas had been constructed along one side of North Street, but the "common" land is still being farmed as demonstrated by the remaining half of the hayrick on the right, but in forty years or so it will form the major part of the grounds of the *Sir Bernard Lovell School* c1925.

Number 11 in the 1914 series of picture postcards shows the High Street end of North Street on a bright summers day, with not a soul to be seen, not a car in sight, and open fields in the background. Only the left hand side of the road can boast a pavement, mainly because there are hardly any houses on the right. Note the "front parlour" shop on the left under the tree, almost certainly a small general store selling anything from buttons to butter, material to marmalade, and still the owner was able to give a service and make a profit.

In this instance the position of the camera has been moved back to expose a slightly more panoramic view of North Street, and whilst this picture is around eleven years or so later than the previous one, there is still an absence of any traffic and/or pedestrians, and a right-hand pavement c1925.

The High Street end of North Street showing the original cottages before all of the spare land was in filled. Above looking across from the High Street, and a close-up of a pair of cottages, whilst bottom right is the road junction crossed with long shadows caused by the winter sunshine. All three pictures were taken on the 14th December 1986.

The position of this row of poplars that flanked the driveway to Upwards Farm can be determined from the picture of Cowhorn Hill on page 3. Almost in line with the West Street end of Westcourt Drive, the area in front of these trees contained for many years the village cricket pitch, and is now the site of the western end of Westlands Avenue c1914.

Below are the local shops in Westcourt Drive as seen on the 2nd March 1986, the Kiosks, the Spar, Courtair the hairdressers, and Mr Rogers the local hardware store, that always seemed to have so much, "out the back." During recent refurbishment the following shop sign came to light that will no doubt bring back memories of the 1960's when Matchbox cars and lorries could be purchased for 2/6d [12½ p]

During the late 1950's plans were agreed to turn a large stretch of farmland, and the local cricket pitch into a housing estate through which would run a sweeping road from which other roads could branch. This is the "dip" in Westcourt Drive with its junction with Henfield Crescent on the 6th June 1999. Below is Westcourt Drive under construction in 1961, whilst to the left is the 1994 version of the same view as you look towards Court Road.

Westcourt Drive as it sweeps past Henfield Crescent. Although the picture, which was taken in March 1986, is only twenty years old, there is still a marked difference in the amount of traffic depicted when compared to the much higher level experienced today.

The last of the small independent "milkmen" D Bryant on his round at the junction of Henfield Crescent and Brooklea, on the 22 February 1986

Henfield Crescent 6 June 1999 whilst below is a similar view of the Crescent and its many inhabitants celebrating with a street party the Queen's Silver Jubilee in June 1977. At the table are Stuart Lewis; Andrew Macdowell; Paul Pidgeon; Lisa Bryer; Paul Lawrence. Amongst the adults are Brenda Lawrence, Mrs Harris and Mr Godden.

Another selection of the Silver Jubilee party held in Henfield Crescent, with some of the children [above] showing off their fancy hats including Jill Bishop on the right, Rachel Noble and Kathryn Glover. The disco is about to get ready, top right, whilst bottom right games are underway on the green with Michelle George; Tania Glover; Julie Nowell; Ian Macdowell; Stephen Nowell; Paul Lawrence; Vicky Blake; Claire Fitzgerald and Rachael Noble.

Although the publisher of this card has again misquoted the name of the view, this is without doubt the circa 1910 rural aspect of Oldland Vale, looking along a much tidier than present Church Lane, with the Warmley Brook crossed, in the foreground, by the ancient clapper bridge. Behind the bridge is the old washhouse used by the Court Road cottagers, and beyond the cluster of cottages that faced on to the brook near School Lane can be seen.

This is the reverse view of the above picture from past the clapper bridge. Behind the family is an old cottage locally known as the Bowler Hat Cottage on the grounds that this type of headwear was once made there. Partially hidden by the trees on the right is the old Pound keeper's house, and across the road beside the bridge can be made out the "beach" used by the inhabitants of both cottages to collect water from the stream, and to use as a place to wash clothes c1905.

A wonderfully composed picture of Mr Pitman, baker of Cadbury Heath, with his basket nonchalantly thrown over his shoulder as he stands by his horse-drawn delivery van in the High Street. Part of the Tabernacle Chapel can be seen on the extreme left c1925.

In this 1930's view of a deserted High Street looking from the *Cherry Tree,* there are just two vehicles and both of those are parked, including the Ford 5cwt delivery van left virtually in the middle of the road, at the junction where West Street joins High Street. By the length of the shadows, this picture would seem to have been taken around midday on a bright summer's day, but perhaps there was a "nip" in the air, according to the dress of both the ladies.

On the right the High Street is in an even more tranquil mood with not a vehicle of any description in sight, and just two gentlemen to distract the photographer's concentration. Note the pleasant absence of the hideous street furniture thrust upon us in today's world, and how neat and tidy it all once was c1922

Above, looking along the High Street from the junction with West Street in the summer of 1914, just one Farm cart occupies an otherwise deserted road. Some of the buildings on the right form the station for the local constabulary. In contrast, below traffic in West Street is congested, as it has to wait before it can pull out into a much busicr High Street on the 26 May 1990.

In one of its many guises, the above picture shows the building on the corner of The Clamp and High Street at the time when it was in the proud possession of Mr & Mrs Adams, who are seen outside their Boot Stores around 1906

Since the previous picture was taken, some twenty years and a World War have passed, and although Mr & Mrs M L Adams still own the business, it has now expanded and includes the local sub post office. Note the attractive public telephone box on the left and the wall-mounted letterbox by the window. Two young boys are happy to compliment the picture, as does the pushbike, and the Royal Enfield V twin motorcycle AM 5463 c1924

A sleepy High Street frozen in time, with just three or four local residents in view, together with a trader's horse and cart waiting patiently for the owners return. M L Adams is still the proprietor of the combined Boot and Shoe shop with post office c 1926

A group of Victorian children are captured on film outside A A Adams' [no relation to M L Adams] general stores with post office. Note the little girl in white blouse with hoop, and the young lady beside her carrying milk home. Despite the fact that the post office was transferred across the road, the Adams' shop continued well into the 1960's selling anything from cooked beetroot to galvanized baths. In the background is the Tabernacle, built in 1811. This picture has been taken from a post card used as a Birthday Card in December 1904.

Opposite is a picture taken in 1996 showing the same view after the destruction of A A Adams' shop and home.

With The Clamp off to the left, this is a rare Sunday view of the High Street. On the right is A A Adams' general store and post office, with the proprietor himself just about to step out onto the pavement sporting a bowler hat and carrying a rolled-up umbrella. Further along a sole cyclist is comfortable as he perambulates along in the middle of the road dodging the after effects of horse drawn traffic. Ahead of him an elderly woman in a long white skirt and a large soft brimmed bonnet crosses the road, with no rush and with no hurry, what a peaceful place Oldland Common once was. Used as a Christmas card, picture c1910

A view that can perhaps be regarded as the hub of the High Street, with the Victorian Villas standing proudly on the left protected by well constructed stonewalls, and with the road and pavement neatly swept. Opposite, a lady with a splendid three wheeled Bath Chair containing a young boy is about to cross the road, having no doubt passed the time of day with the two gentlemen outside the *Old Castle* off licence, with its big sign advertising Rogers Ales. This frozen moment took place in the summer of 1914, just prior to when the world was about to change forever.

The bright winter sunshine falls across a corner of the High Street Post Office, whilst just beyond a family group, wrapped up against the cold air have crossed the top of Castle Street, and the sign pointing to Oldland FC. 29th January 1984.

Covered with a light dusting of snow is Golding, the original and at one time only Fish & Chip shop in the village attached to the High Street cottage, the home of the proprietor and master fryer, 20th January 1985.

In contrast to the picture on page 40 which was taken by the same photographer, when he set up his apparatus to capture the High Street in the reverse direction, he attracted a much larger audience with no less than 10 cloth-capped men prepared to see what was going on, plus a rather elderly gentleman with flowing white whiskers. A little more shyly two or three young ladies and girls add to this interesting scene. Behind the girls in the white dresses, on the left is the *Old Castle* off licence. As they all appear to be wearing their best clothes this is probably another Sunday picture most likely taken on the same day as the earlier picture c1910.

We have with the camera now moved further along the High Street both in distance and in time. Cars are still something of a rarity and the Morris BHT 700 has no difficulty in finding a convenient place to park. Although only just visible, a brewery lorry is outside the *Dolphin Inn,* whilst across the road the owner of the right-hand detached house has opened up a small shop next to the bay-windowed room, c1935

On the right is roughly the same view as seen in 1996 showing how much busier Oldland has become over the past sixty years

The relatively newly constructed *Dolphin Inn,* a George's Brewery tied house built at the other end of the High Street as the fourth public house in the village. On the opposite side of the road a group of young ladies stand idly outside the local corset factory, as they watch the antics of the photographer, whilst behind them a solitary man stands where North Street joins High Street, note the large house facing onto the former road. Beyond the inn is an open field, and behind the sign is a large mansion facing Redfield Edge, with to its left is what would appear to be an old substantial farmhouse, note also the tar boiler to the left of the sign. Taken during the summer of 1914, being number six in a series of twelve pictures of the village that were probably photographed on the same day.

From an early picture taken before the outbreak of the First World War to a reverse view of the High Street taken after the Second World War, so much has changed and yet so little is different. The same properties still face onto a traffic free road, now lined with telegraph poles and overhead wires, but it will only be another decade or two before the peace and calm will be broken forever, c1955.

Three pictures showing examples of the specialist motor vehicle bodybuilding work carried out during the 1950/60's by the Oldland Motor Body Builders Ltd. All pictures c1962.

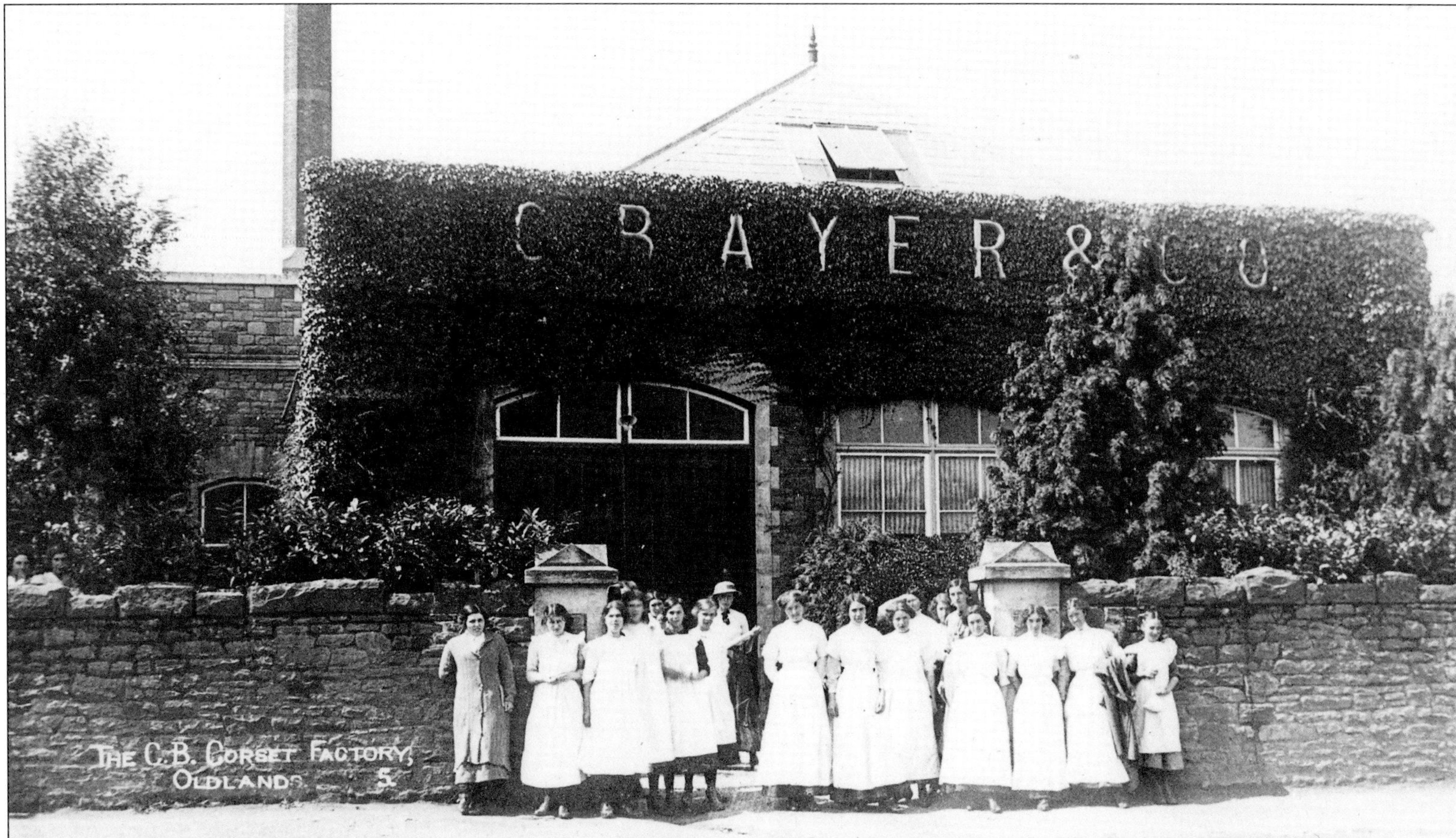

During the Edwardian period fashionable women had their figures shaped by the artificial means of squeezing themselves into extra long tight fitting corsets, which forced the bust forward and the bottom out to create an 'S' shape, with an achievable 17/18 inch waist. However, corsets were not confined to the upper class, even female servants were obliged to wear corsets, despite the fact that it made it very difficult for the servant to bend down when carrying out her duties. Above we have the ladies who helped produce those items of torture standing outside C Bayer & Company's Corset Factory in the High Street. Nearly all are dressed in white and some may by wearing corsets, with "matron," in what appears to be a white bowler hat standing at the back, whilst three women who are, perhaps, not in such clean white dresses hide their bodies behind the wall c1914.

Top left is the ivy-covered building of C Bayer & Co as seen on the previous page, having by now become the office and showroom of Simplex, manufactures of sectional bookcases, storage units and TV display cabinets c1996. The remaining three pictures show the progress being made in 2005 after the site had been cleared and the start of the construction of houses in what is to become "Trescothick Court"

In the almost traffic free environment of the day it was perfectly safe for the photographer to arrange no less than fourteen men and boys across the bend in the road. All are perfectly relaxed having adopted their own particular pose to stand as still as possible whilst perhaps not realising that this moment in time would be frozen for ever, and allow us a small glimpse into a world that is so different from our own. Note the substantial farmhouse behind the group to the right of the picture c1910.

Safely around the bend with the one exception of a small handcart at the side of the road, we can witness an apparently abandoned High Street, as it reaches out, past a row of Victorian terraced houses, towards the corrugated chapel c1925.

The shadows caused by the evening sun spread themselves across a different view of a traffic free High Street as the photographer has attracted and arranged another group, this time of nine men, of whom one is holding a staff, one, with a straw boater, has a bicycle, whereas another has a cricket bat. As for the females, two are sheltering behind the men, whilst a third hides behind a gatepost c1910.

Above three children are a little self conscious as they wait for the picture to be taken, watched by a young girl with small child in a pram c1924
Top right: St Anne's stands proudly on its hill at a time when there was a pride in keeping the approach roads/paths neat and tidy.

Above on the right the local vicar is surrounded by a large group of ladies all dressed for a pageant based upon the British Empire. Fourth left in back row is Lavinia Saunders, can you recognise anyone else? Photographed on the vicarage lawn c1920.

Unfortunately very little is known of the group photograph on the left, except it is believed to be the Warmley AFC team c1912. Please let the Author know, if you are able to recognize anyone in the photograph.

As with the picture above little is know about this picture other than it is also the Warmley Football Team c1935, and that two of the players are Les Cull, and William [Bill] Shipp.

A quartet of team photographs, l/r. Oldland FC 1910, no one identified; Oldland FC 1946, back row ~ Lewis; Fussell; Mortimore; Stone; Taylor; Gardiner; Ollis; Lambden; Joy; Bush; Taylor; front row Withers; Tippett; Curtis; King; Needs; Lucas; Nicholls; Teal; and Anstey.
St Annes AFC, feature in the bottom row with the l/h one taken c1922 and the r/h in 1921. In the back line is Ollie Gerrish and Albert Williams, the first three in the middle are Jack Gerrish; Pete Gibbs and Courtney May, with the ball is Lewis White, and on the right is Howard Hillier.

Oldland Youth Club Party wait outside the Church Hall to have their group photograph before leaving for a trip to Starsdelt in Germany July 1955, front row l/r: T Dando; A Campbell; M Smailes; C Smailes; Mrs C Isaacs; J Clothier and K Sweet. Back row; l/r not known; D Mortimer; Mr R Isaacs; L Always; J Sawyer, and G Beese

Members of the Oldland Common youth club have all gathered together for a celebratory photograph in the Church Hall c1956.

The newly constructed Church Hall built on land facing School Lane, and dwarfing the adjacent row of cottages, now all sadly demolished. Used as a birthday card on the 2nd August 1914, this view could only have been a matter of weeks old at that time. On the right is a picture showing the frontage of the Church Hall after an 18-ton lorry, carrying paint had overturned whilst negotiating the bend on the 1st September 1983.

The Church Hall from a different angle showing the chimneystack rising from the original kitchen area, subsequently removed when the hall was converted to a modest form of central heating. In this picture the photographer appears to have persuaded a group of painters and decorators to pose for the camera. Note gentleman in middle of the group holding rolls of wallpaper, the old gas light behind the second man in on the right, and the fact that the photographer is standing on the countryside of the field wall c1925.

A rather deserted Barry Road looking towards the village some years before the construction of St Annes Drive, showing the well built stone villas on the left, whilst in the background the houses between West Street and the Clamp can be seen c1925

With *Oaklands* desperately trying to hide itself behind the branches of the trees, this view of Barry Road is more panoramic than the previous picture, and centrally includes what must have been regarded at the time as quite modern looking houses. The well-maintained field wall and ditch on the right stands out very favourably with today's tangle and unkempt appearance and there is still no sign of St Annes Drive c1933.

Looking back towards the village from the field adjacent to Barry Road showing, along the road and behind the trees, the many villas built during the latter decade or two of the nineteenth century. Cattle from Park Farm graze in the field, and apart from the traffic, this is one area of Oldland that on the surface has not dramatically changed over the years although the same cannot be said about the land behind the houses, which now contains a substantial housing estate and primary school, c1926

Barry Road when life was a little more tranquil. Electricity has arrived, even if the motorcar has not yet ousted the equine power of the past c1924,

Back to West Street, showing one of the older cottages and the village store, 16th May 1987

Below is a picture of the "Hatters of Oldland" c1880. Although the exact location has not been positively identified it is believed to be outside a cottage in West Street. The tall gentleman in the middle is Reuben Jefferies, whose occupation in the 1841 census ~ when he was 35 years old, is shown as a Hat maker.

The man standing third from right is George Jefferies, whilst to his left is Hester Jefferies, unfortunately none of the others have yet been positively identified. Reproduced by kind permission of Rosemary Rainbird.

The above family group was almost certainly taken around 1900 in the garden of "Oaklands" 50 Barry Road, the home of Albert Jefferies who is seen on the left of the back-row, with Jesse Fudge and Frederick Jefferies. Seated l/r are Mr Rex; Frederick [Albert's son]; Annie [Frederick's wife, with their son George]; Lucy [Albert's wife]; and Mrs Rex. The children are Flo Rex; Emmie and Maud Jefferies; and Tom Rex. The right-hand pictures both depict children at Oldland Common Council School, with at the top Blanche; Reggie; Elsie and Billy Shipp amongst their 1913 classmates. Although we are told that the lower picture was taken in 1909, unfortunately none of the children have been identified.

On the left are two pictures of the staff and pupils of Oldland Common Council School in 1910, but as with other pictures, at present all remain anonymous. Above is "Slade's Cottage in need of renovation, School Road February 1986.

The abandoned "Mrs Worlock's Cottage" in School Lane, having been hit by time, decay and vandals, February 1986.

The same cottage, different angle as seen 3 May 1987.